AMERICA,
I Hear You

AMERICA, I Hear You

A Story about George Gershwin

by Barbara Mitchell

illustrations by Jan Hosking Smith

A Carolrhoda Creative Minds Book

Carolrhoda Books, Inc./Minneapolis

8652

For Don Hetrick and Rudy DiFelice—
my Hambitzer and Kilenyi

LIBRARY OF CONGRESS CATALOGING-IN-PUBLICATION DATA

Mitchell, Barbara, 1941-
   America, I hear you.

   (A Carolrhoda creative minds book)
   Summary: Focuses on the life and musical career
of the composer who wrote a number of popular
musicals and brought jazz into the realm of acceptable
and respectable music.
   1. Gershwin, George, 1898-1937—Juvenile literature.
2. Composers—United States—Biography—Juvenile
literature. [1. Gershwin, George, 1898-1937.
2. Composers] I. Hosking Smith, Jan, ill. II. Title.
III. Series.
ML410.G288M6   1987   780'.92'4 [B] [92]   87-6544
ISBN 0-87614-309-5 (lib. bdg.)

Manufactured in the United States of America

   2   3   4   5   6   7   8   9   10   97   96   95   94   93   92   91   90   89   88

Table of Contents

ACKNOWLEDGMENTS

I would like to thank Mr. Charles Sens and Mr. Wayne Shirley of the Library of Congress for sharing the George Gershwin Collection with me.

Mr. Sens provided Gershwin family letters and numerous newspaper clippings. He allowed me to sit at the desk designed by Gershwin himself and to explore its drawers and cubbyholes.

Mr. Shirley, considered the nation's top Gershwin expert, answered questions, recalled "icing-on-the-cake" anecdotes, and placed Gershwin's student notebooks and handsomely bound original of *Rhapsody in Blue* in my hands.

The Library of Congress is now in the process of creating a George Gershwin room, a place where people will be able to visit and share in the treasures given to us by this very special American composer.

Chapter One

George Gershvin handed his mother a pair of well-used roller skates. Mrs. Gershvin took the precious possession held out by her eight-year-old son and laid them gently in the box marked GEORGE.

It was 1906, and the Gershvins were moving to New York City's Lower East Side. The Gershvins were *always* moving. Rose and Morris Gershvin were Russian Jewish immigrants who had come to New York during the 1890s. New York was full of business opportunities, and Morris Gershvin kept his family busy hopping from the East Side, to Brooklyn, back to the East Side, out to Coney

Island, over to Harlem in order to take advantage of those opportunities. A businessman should live in the same neighborhood as his customers, Morris Gershvin believed.

Rose Gershvin was not so sure about all the moving. Each move meant a new school for her children and new friends to make. But one thing George never had a problem with was making friends. George was adventurous.

No sooner were the packing boxes set down than George was strapping on his roller skates to explore the new neighborhood. In a matter of days, he was a friend of the policeman on the corner, and the mothers calling out of crowded tenement houses to their children below soon knew George's name as well.

Before long, George discovered that skating down the Lower East Side streets was tricky. There were the pushcarts full of fruits and vegetables to weave around. There were the games of street hockey and punch ball to plow through. Many of the East Side boys were rough and ready. George often found himself in the midst of a brawl, skates and all. No matter. The new whiz on skates could fight his way through the streets if necessary, and he was soon accepted as "the champ."

The thing George liked best about the East Side, though, was listening to the sounds—city sounds. The "el" train roared above the streets, shaking the windows of the Gershvin apartment. The cries of the street vendors and the many voices of the neighbors chatting in Italian, Gaelic, Polish, and Yiddish filled George's ears.

In Harlem, one of his favorite jaunts, George soon found a new pastime. He would sit on the curb outside the *Baron Wilkins Club*, a dance hall that eight-year-old George had no hope of getting into. There the loud, exciting rhythms of the Jim Europe Band made their way out to him. The band played a music new to New York— ragtime. The "raggers," men who had come up from Mississippi riverboat towns, built their rhythmic, "bluesy" sound on black dance music. George just couldn't seem to get the music out of his head.

On a spring afternoon in 1908, George discovered yet another kind of music—classical music. The entire student body of Public School No. 25 had been ushered into the auditorium. Everybody, that is, but George Gershvin. George was out throwing a ball against the side of the building.

The entertainment had been announced that

morning. A violin concert by a third-grade violinist. Jazzy, bluesy music on a street curb was one thing, but a school violin concert? George was determined not to attend. George was like that—headstrong. His frustrated teachers were forever marching him to the principal's office for one reason or another.

Determined as he was to avoid the concert, George could not help but hear the music as it floated out the school windows. Young Maxie Rosenzweig did not play the blues. Maxie played Mozart, Beethoven, Dvořák—and much to his amazement George found himself listening. The pure, liquid tones pouring out of Rosenzweig's violin were touching George deep down inside. They were, as he was to say years later, "a flashing revelation of beauty."

George had planned to slip away as soon as possible after school and get into his roller skates. Instead he found himself standing by the third-grade exit waiting for school to let out. He *had* to meet the creator of those beautiful sounds.

The third graders came tumbling out of their exit, but not one of them carried a violin case. George hung around for another half hour—still no violinist. As it turned out, the tired performer

had been picked up by his mother at the teachers' exit. George marched himself to the principal's office (without any help, for once) and asked for the violinist's name. He went over to the Rosenzweig house, knocked on the door, and introduced himself.

George and Maxie were soon spending hours together talking about music. Maxie really knew his music. He would grow up to be Max Rosen, a famous violinist.

Dance-hall music. Concert-hall music. Sound-loving George was fascinated by it all. He began spending much of his allowance at penny arcades, where automatic pianos, called "players," magically rolled out the latest hit songs. He also made a new friend at this time—a friend whose family owned a piano.

When George was 12, Mrs. Gershvin decided it was time the family had a piano. She thought that music might help George's older brother, Ira, overcome his shyness.

Ira, it turned out, did not care a bit about the piano. Ira's love was reading. George cared, though. He sat down at once and played his mother a tune he had picked out on his friend's piano. So it was George who ended up with piano lessons.

One by one, George went through four neighborhood piano teachers. The lessons were all the same, he found. He twirled the piano stool to his height at the big old upright. He ran over the scales. He played a couple of ditties from the exercise book. He paid his $.50 and went home. That was it. A piano lesson ought to be *more*, George thought.

Then George heard about Charles Hambitzer. Hambitzer was known to be a fine piano teacher. He also composed and played with the elegant Waldorf-Astoria Hotel's orchestra.

"Play for me," Hambitzer said when George appeared for the first time at his studio.

George sat down and played his latest lesson piece.

Hambitzer shook his head. The music coming out of his grand piano was sadly lacking. "Who in the world taught you to play like that?" the master teacher demanded.

George told Hambitzer about the first four piano teachers.

This boy was serious about music. Hambitzer could feel it. "Here you will learn to play *music*," he said. He loaded George down with fat books on piano technique and music of the masters.

"I am going to work you as you have never been worked before," he told his new student.

Hambitzer was a live wire. He paced the studio as George went through the rigorous exercises in technique. "FIX IT!" Hambitzer exclaimed when George played a sloppy phrase.

Then Hambitzer would sit on the bench beside his intent young student. "That's it, George... like molasses...now, sparkle. Make that piano talk, George."

So there *was* more to piano lessons, just as George had sensed. There was music in the soul of George Gershvin, and Hambitzer was bringing it out. George was crazy about this exciting new teacher.

There was just one thing that bothered him about his lessons with Hambitzer, and George made up his mind to say something about it. "I want to play *modern* music," he informed his teacher after a lesson heavy on the formal classical music of Liszt and Chopin.

At his next lesson, there was a new piece of music waiting on the piano for George—a composition by Maurice Ravel, France's "wild new modernist." Hambitzer winked. "A compromise," he said. George happily sat down at the piano.

George didn't forget about his love for ragtime music, either. There was a new ragtime song that was all the rage—Irving Berlin's "Alexander's Ragtime Band." The Gershvin apartment was just as likely to ring with the snappy rhythms of Berlin as with Liszt preludes these days.

While George was busy learning to play the piano, his mother enrolled him in the High School of Commerce. The Gershvin men had been businessmen for generations. George was nearly 15 now, and it was time he began learning some business skills. George didn't fill his dull gray bookkeeper's ledgers with columns of numbers, though. He neatly pasted them from cover to cover with pictures of composers and performers that he had cut out of concert programs and newspapers.

One afternoon George came home from the High School of Commerce with a shocking announcement. "I want to quit school, Mama," he said. "I am going to get a job with a music publisher and learn to write songs."

George waited for this to sink in. "I am going to be a composer," he continued.

Rose Gershvin looked into the dark, dreamy looking eyes that gazed back into her own. Music was fine for enjoyment, but could her son make a living from it? She doubted it.

"Well, we shall see what Papa has to say about this," she said at last.

Chapter Two

George did not return to school that September of 1913. Instead he spent his days sitting at a piano at Remick's Publishing Company. Remick's was one of Tin Pan Alley's top music publishers. "The Alley" was actually a New York City street that was lined with song-publishing companies. Performers from Broadway, New York's glamorous street of theaters, made their way from publisher to publisher looking for that magical song that would make their act a hit. Pianos pounded. Trumpets blared. Tap-dance shoes clicked. It all added up to a din louder than tin pans banging together.

George had been hired as a "plugger." His job was to convince the song hunters that they ought to buy songs published by Remick's. Every publisher had its hallway of pluggers. Each player sat in a cubicle at his own piano, pounding out songs that were hot off the presses.

A verse and a chorus, a few basic harmonies, and a dab of old-time sweetness added up to a song. George soon discovered that all the songs on Tin Pan Alley sounded alike. This was definitely not the place to learn how to write *creative* songs. He took his problem to his piano teacher.

"What you need is some study with a real master of composition and orchestration," Hambitzer told him. Hambitzer convinced his friend Edward Kilenyi to take George on as a student. Kilenyi played violin with the Waldorf-Astoria orchestra. The Hungarian-born musician was also a highly respected teacher. Kilenyi started George out by teaching him the European standards for harmonizing songs based on the chords of the eight-tone scale. George dutifully took all this down in a music theory workbook his teacher provided.

"This is *devilish* hard," George complained after he'd spent a whole evening struggling with a difficult chord progression.

Kilenyi looked over the lesson. "Devilish hard, you say?" he wrote in George's workbook. George had mastered European-style harmonizing to perfection.

Then George happily went about *breaking* the centuries-old rules. He made new, unheard-of chord progressions. He put in flatted notes where they hadn't been before. The result was a brand new sound—a Gershvin sound.

One week George arrived at Kilenyi's to find a concert clarinetist waiting to play for him. "It is time we began the art of orchestration," Kilenyi explained.

"Orchestration—deciding what instruments will play your compositions—is like using a box of paints, George," Kilenyi said. "Each instrument has its own color. The way you mix these sound-colors is what makes your music really yours." The next week there was a trombonist present, then a percussionist. Kilenyi did not do this for every student, but he wanted George to know the orchestral family as well as he knew his own family. George was so talented that Kilenyi wanted to help him in every way he could.

George did his orchestration lessons every bit as carefully as those he had done in his theory book. He also began to write little arrangements of his own in the margins. These arrangements captured the jazzy, bluesy sounds George remembered from the Harlem raggers. Kilenyi was pleased with George's extra efforts. His special protégé was starting to take off on his own.

It was not long before George was beginning to work these new sounds he was creating into songs. In between Remick songs, he began to play Gershvin songs. His boss's musical ear picked up the new sounds at once, of course, and Mose Gumble was not pleased. "I hired you to play Remick songs," he said.

George felt it was time to move on and went to the Harms Publishing Company. His new boss saw right away that he had acquired a gem. This youngest plugger on Tin Pan Alley sparkled at the piano, and the Gershvin cubicle was always crowded with song hunters. George's own compositions and the compositions published by Harms —played in the Gershvin style—went straight to the hearts of the buyers. What was more, the boy had charm—every bit as important to selling songs as piano playing. "Work whatever hours you want," the happy president of Harms declared. "Just keep playing those songs of yours."

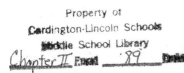

Looking over George's shoulder one day was a young man named Irving Ceasar. "Do those songs of yours have words?" he asked.

"Not yet," George said.

Ceasar went on to explain that he was a lyricist. He worked for Ford Motor Company, but his real interest was writing words to songs.

"Meet me at Dinty Moore's at noon," George said as he went back to his work.

"Dinty's" was a lunch counter where Broadway stars and hopefuls often ate. Over the owner's famous onion-filled hamburgers, George and Irving talked about music. Almost at once, they found themselves putting their ideas together for a song.

George and Irving hopped on a bus that would take them to the Gershvin apartment. The double-decker omnibus threaded its way through a curious mixture of horse-drawn hansom cabs and shiny new automobiles. New York was becoming more modern every day.

"Music ought to reflect its own time," George remarked. Irving agreed.

The bus picked up speed as it headed out toward the Gershvin home, now in Washington Heights. The rhythmic spin of its wheels and the

busy, bird's-eye view from the top deck inspired George Gershvin. By the time they got off the bus, a rollicking rhythm was dancing in his head. The song he and Irving had talked over at lunch was already taking shape.

George took the apartment steps three at a time. Irving followed close behind. They went straight to the piano and began hammering out their new song. By the end of the afternoon, "Swanee" was created.

George and Irving wanted their song to be heard by the public. The conductor of Capitol Theatre's orchestra liked the song and introduced it with his band. The audience, however, was unimpressed. It was the custom for a new song's publisher to offer copies of the song for sale at the end of a show. Sheet music hawkers worked their way through the home-going crowd. "'Swanee,' right here! Get your copy now!" George and Irving hovered nervously on the sidelines. There were so few buyers that it was embarrassing.

"Swanee" would have met an early death had not Broadway star Al Jolson come upon it one night at a party where the fun-loving, fast-rising composer was also a guest. George, as usual, had ended up at the piano playing his latest musical inspirations. Jolson's sharp ear picked up "Swanee's" charm at once. "Play that again, Gershvin!" he demanded.

Jolson was captivated. The song had a fascinating rhythm, subtle mood change—everything a song should have. He sang it himself at one of his Sunday night shows. Jolson gave "Swanee" everything he had. The startled audience could not help but be caught up in it. After that, "Swanee" sold a million sheet music copies and two million records within the year. George's first real hit song had taken life.

While George had been wrapped up in his music, his book-loving brother Ira had been carrying on a quiet writing career. His poems had begun to appear in literary magazines. "You know," said George one day, "we really ought to start putting our talents together." Ira thought it was a good idea, too.

Once the Gershvin brothers started turning out joint songs, there was no stopping them. Ira's clever lyrics and George's sparkling, animated rhythms and harmonies reflected the America they saw every day and caught the attention of Broadway in no time. Since we're writing American music, the Gershvins thought, why not become

more American ourselves. It's time we Americanized our old-world name. The entire Gershvin family changed their name to Gershwin.

The most glamorous Broadway shows of the early 1900s were the Ziegfeld Follies. Footlights would illuminate the stage. A starlit stairway would appear, lined with beautiful showgirls descending to "A Pretty Girl Is Like a Melody." Florenz Ziegfeld had a competitor named George White, who believed a good show needed more than just pretty girls. It needed music that *spoke* to the audience. He cleverly engaged George and Ira to do his new shows known as the Scandals. Soon cabbies were whistling the Gershwin brothers' "Fascinating Rhythm." Waitresses were humming "Somebody Loves Me." Mothers and fathers across America put their children to bed, turned the lights down low, and put "The Man I Love" on the phonograph. The word was out— Gershwin songs were touched by magic.

Chapter Three

George and Ira Gershwin were having coffee one morning soon after New Year's Day in 1924. "Listen to this!" Ira said.

Ira was reading the New York *Herald Tribune*. A small item on the arts page had jumped out at him. He began to read. "George Gershwin is at work on a concerto for Paul Whiteman's 'Experiment in Jazz' to be performed February 12."

George set down his coffee cup. Today was January 4. Both he and Ira knew full well that there was no such work in progress.

George got on the phone to the dance-band king. "Listen, Whiteman, I never actually *said* I would do that jazz piano concerto we talked about," he said. "I've got four musicals in the making."

"*You* can do it, George," said Whiteman. "I'll send Grofé over to lend a hand." Whiteman hung up.

The idea of the "experiment" was to prove that jazz was worthy of being played on the American concert stage. Whiteman had planned a concert that would cover jazz from its earliest beginnings with black musicians to the present. America's classical musicians did not think jazz measured up to their own "serious" music. They thought it had no form. Why, jazz wasn't even written down half the time, they argued. Players simply stood up and took a free-swinging "ride" on their instruments.

Whiteman, though, took jazz seriously and was thinking of new ways to present it to the public. He had gone so far as to add violins to his own dance band. Gershwin's ideas went further still. Why not combine the freedom of jazz and the strict guidelines of classical form to create a sophisticated *new* sound? The idea intrigued him.

George was about to leave for Boston to rehearse his new musical, *Sweet Little Devil.* Into his suitcase went some score paper. The astonishing news in print was not about to get the best of energetic George Gershwin. He stretched out on the train seat, the music-writing paper spread across his knees. As the train rocked its way northward, he got down to organizing the scrap of a musical theme that was floating around in his head.

By the time the train pulled into Boston, George had a plan for an American rhapsody, a kaleidoscope of American life. It was to become his *Rhapsody in Blue.* Composing a major work for solo piano and orchestra aboard a rattle-banging train did not bother George in the least. "I frequently hear music in the midst of noise," he said.

A week after his return to New York, George had a rough piano score finished for his rhapsody. Now he had to create the orchestral support for his new composition. Ferde Grofé, Whiteman's top-notch orchestral arranger, practically moved into the Gershwin apartment. Gershwin knew just what he wanted the opening of his rhapsody to say and how to say it.

He penciled in a solo for clarinet that began with a trill in the instrument's warm, low register. The trill led into a "glissando," a slide all the way up to the clarinet's brilliant high range.

Grofé took one look at the long "gliss" and let out a whistle. Tricky business, this. It would require the clarinetist to glide his fingers just so over the keys and to have superb control over the reed. Otherwise, the impressive slide would end up as a choke.

Gershwin set down the cigar he liked to puff on while hard at work and smiled. He knew that Ross Gorman, Whiteman's clarinetist, could carry it off.

The afternoon of the "Experiment in Jazz" arrived; miraculously, Gershwin's score was ready. Aeolian Hall was packed with concertgoers.

The curtain went up. Whiteman stood at center stage, flanked by his band. Seated in the front row of the audience were New York City's top music critics. The experienced conductor had a sudden case of stage jitters. Suppose the experiment did *not* work. Whiteman gave a short introductory talk on the history of jazz. Then the experiment began. It was to be a long one. The elegant purple and gold program listed 24 numbers. Gershwin and his rhapsody would appear next to last. By intermission, it was clear that the audience was tiring of its education in jazz.

Gershwin strode onstage at last, looking cool and collected. He sat down at the piano and gave Whiteman a nod. Gorman took up his clarinet. He worked into Gershwin's warm, low trill. The trill shivered with excitement, then blossomed into a perfectly executed glissando. The audience sat up. Gershwin and Gorman exchanged a wink. They had done just what they had set out to do.

George Gershwin sat waiting for the piano entrance, looking every bit as though he were at home in his own living room. From the orchestra came the kaleidoscope of hustling-bustling, growing America that Gershwin had envisioned. The sounds of old-world Yiddish folk songs, hot jazz, and tender blues all came together in that sophisticated *new* sound that George Gershwin was hoping for. They made a sound that mirrored the soul of their composer—that Gershwin sound.

Orchestra and piano took off together like a train barreling out of Grand Central Station. The audience was fully awake now. They were completely caught up in the music as it took them through mood after mood—playfulness,

nostalgia, tenderness—before finishing with a pulsating finale. When the rhapsody was over, the audience gave an ovation that lasted ten minutes.

The judgments handed down by the critics came out in the morning news. Some were favorable. Some were not. It didn't matter, though. The audience had fallen in love with *Rhapsody in Blue*—and with its composer as well.

Symphonic jazz was on the American concert stage to stay. The proof came when Walter Damrosch invited Gershwin to compose a concerto for his orchestra. As conductor of the New York Symphony Society, Damrosch was considered America's top musical figure. George named his new concerto the *New York* Concerto.

Rhapsody in Blue had turned its composer into THE George Gershwin. There was no need for Rose Gershwin to worry about George making a living in music now. The Gershwin family moved into a new, larger house that quickly became a gathering spot for music lovers. The real fascination was the fifth floor—George's private apartment.

George had taken care to make his personal rooms warm and inviting. The room in which he did his composing held a brick fireplace, his grand piano, and a number of cozy chairs.

George Gershwin loved people. He never re-fused a visitor, even when he was in the middle of a new composition. Still, there were deadlines to be met. George and Ira were at work on the musicals *Oh, Kay!* and *Treasure Girl* at this time. George took to writing into the wee hours of the night and sleeping in the mornings. At times, he actually had to take a room in the hotel around the corner in order to work uninterrupted.

When George really felt the need to get out of the limelight, he would take off for Paris. "There's a city I could write about," he said. George walked all over Paris, exploring everything from quiet cafés to the grand cathedral of Notre Dame. He found it all charming.

It was neither grand cathedrals nor sidewalk cafés that George Gershwin was exploring one summer afternoon in 1928, though. He and Polish composer Alexandre Tansman were puttering about in grimy Parisian junkyards and dusty second-hand shops. Gershwin was looking for something in particular—old Parisian taxi horns.

"What on earth do you want with the rusty old things?" Tansman asked.

George smiled mysteriously. "I have need of them," he said.

The American composer began spending many hours in his hotel room. He was at work on a new composition. "It's the most modern thing I've done yet!" he told Tansman happily.

Tansman noticed that a change had come over his friend. When they walked the wide boulevards crammed with honking automobiles, Gershwin's face would take on a nostalgic look. The Parisian streets reminded him of something—home. Did all this have to do with the mysterious new composition? Tansman wondered.

Gershwin's *An American in Paris* was introduced the following December at Carnegie Hall. George had written in the program notes that his purpose for this new music was to give an impression of how an American might feel while in Paris. The music began with a sauntering walking theme. George had always felt that walking was the way to see Paris. The orchestra's percussion section suddenly became busy. There was a most unusual set of drummers' traps in front of them tonight—real Parisian taxi horns. The horns had been lugged all the way from Europe, tucked into Gershwin's suitcases.

HONK-HONK, BEEP-BEEP-BEEP! Carnegie Hall took on the sounds of downtown Paris. The audience was entranced. The critics were floored. HORNS honking at Carnegie! Up to now, Carnegie Hall had been a place where only classical music had been performed.

The horns quieted. On came a soft touch of the blues. The American visitor had stopped at a café for a cooling drink, perhaps. The music turned nostalgic. Paris had charm, but it was not home. The music made the listeners feel what the composer had felt—homesick for hustling-bustling New York.

Chapter Four

By the early 1920s, George Gershwin had written popular songs, a rhapsody, the tone poem that was *An American in Paris*, and Broadway shows. Now there was another musical form that haunted him, the most demanding of all. He had a deep desire to write an opera—an American opera.

One night after a particularly hard day of show rehearsals, George found himself too anxious to sleep. He reached for a book on his night table. The newly published *Porgy* was a love story. Porgy was a crippled beggar in love with a beautiful but weak-willed woman named Bess. The story had tenderness, humor, and a wealth of charm.

George read it straight through and phoned the author that very night. Du Bose Heyward liked the idea of his book being set to music. Gershwin had the story for an opera, but it wasn't until much later that he actually began working on it. The busy New York composer and the far-away Southern writer had trouble getting together.

"Ira, I am going to South Carolina," George announced one December morning in 1933.

"South Carolina, George?" his surprised brother asked. December was the social season in New York. It was odd for party-loving George to leave at such a time.

"Yes," said George. "I'll be staying several months. It's for my opera."

George rented a tiny shack with a screened-in porch on one of the Sea Islands off the coast of South Carolina. The Geechee blacks, descendants of black slaves, lived on these coastal islands. George planned to observe first-hand the life that Porgy had lived.

The rich heritage of African music was still very much alive in the Sea Islands. George sat on his porch taking in the streetcalls of fish and vegetable vendors. The gentle sea breezes blew work chants and centuries-old lullabies his way.

On Sundays, George went to the Geechee church. Island worship was full of the singing of spirituals. The Geechees especially took pride in their "shouts." A circle of men formed, a leader in the middle. The leader began a low chant. Women and children stood on the sidelines, swaying to the soft rhythms. The chant grew stronger. Hands started clapping. Feet started tapping. More and more people would join in the fervent prayer, and the circle of men was soon caught up in a frenzy of movement.

One hot Sunday night, George Gershwin joined the ring. The shout was especially lively that night. Before he knew what was happening, Gershwin found himself in the center. The visitor had so impressed the leader that he had given up his place to George.

George carefully recorded all these impressions. Back to New York they went and into his opera. He had decided to work the spirituals and chants into his own compositions so that the music in his opera would have a unifying theme.

George got so excited about doing the new opera that he designed a desk especially for working on it. The modern mahogany and rose-wood piece of furniture fit his medium-sized

frame to a "T." It fit comfortably into the curve of his Steinway grand piano—so that he could easily turn from composing to playing.

Work on the opera began February 20, 1934. By December of the same year, George had the music completed—all 700 pages of it.

It was party time again, and George was more than ready for some relaxation. Christmas Eve found him getting into his tuxedo. He would end up at the piano, no doubt. That was just fine. George at the piano was George at his happiest. It was there that he could share the deepest part of himself.

The phone rang. The caller was composer Richard Rodgers. He and his wife, Dorothy, would not be able to accompany Gershwin to the party as planned. Dorothy, expecting a baby soon, was not doing well. The doctor had ordered her off her feet.

George quickly exchanged his tux for some casual clothes. He tucked a fat stack of music under his arm and went over to the Rodgers's house. Rodgers turned on the Christmas tree lights. George laid a fire in the fireplace. Together they carried Dorothy to the living room sofa. George lit up a cigar and sat down at the piano.

He proceeded to play *Porgy and Bess*. The December evening was soon full of firelight, "Summertime," and "Bess, You Is My Woman Now."

The Rodgers were the first people ever to hear Gershwin's popular American folk opera. "That was a Christmas Eve we shall never forget," Richard Rodgers later said.

Chapter Five

The 1930s were busy years for George Gershwin. *Porgy and Bess* opened in Boston and shortly after that in New York. During the 30s, he and Ira created four musicals—*Girl Crazy*, *Of Thee I Sing*, *Let 'Em Eat Cake*, and *Strike Up the Band*.

The 30s were not, however, happy years for America. The country was in the midst of the Great Depression. Banks closed. Businesses failed. Many Americans could hardly keep food on the table let alone afford Broadway shows. Instead they found escape from their worries at the cheaper-priced movies.

In 1931, Gershwin was invited to do the musical score for the Twentieth Century Fox film *Delicious*. He and Ira moved to California.

Delicious called for a brief musical description of Manhattan. New York City was alive with the sound of riveters at work on buildings that scraped the sky. George took their racket as his theme.

He then expanded the movie theme into a new rhapsody—*Rhapsody in Rivets.*

In 1935, George was asked to do the score for the film *Shall We Dance.* "You need not bother with the background music, just the main songs," the producer told him.

Gershwin looked the man in the eye. "I want to bother," he said. He spent much of 1936 on the film.

In 1937, George had contracts for the films *A Damsel in Distress* and *The Goldwyn Follies.* Out of *The Goldwyn Follies* came one of his most beautiful songs, "Love Is Here to Stay." It was to be Gershwin's last song.

That same year, the composer-performer was invited to play an all-Gershwin concert with the Los Angeles Philharmonic. While performing his Concerto in F (the *New York* Concerto), George's mind suddenly went blank. He missed a few bars of the music, recovered, and went on with the concert. The experience shook him, though. How could a composer forget his own music?

Medical examinations showed no sign of a problem. "You are overworking yourself. Relax," George's doctors told him. George played tennis. He took walks with his wire-haired terrier, Tony.

He and Ira swam each day in the pool of their new California home. Still, he felt no better. Can all this be nerves? Gershwin wondered.

Early in the summer of 1937, George collapsed at the Goldwyn studio. He had been looking tired and had lost weight. Bright lights had begun to bother his eyes. Further tests revealed no physical problems.

On July 10, Gershwin collapsed yet again. He was rushed to the hospital, where more tests were performed. This time, the results were more conclusive—George Gershwin had a cancerous brain tumor. A delicate operation was performed immediately, but it was too late. Gershwin never regained consciousness. He died the following morning, just months short of his 39th birthday.

The sad news went out to the family and close friends first. Then it hit the headlines—GEORGE GERSHWIN DEAD.

"I don't have to believe it if I don't want to," journalist John O'Hara said.

The truth was, nobody wanted to believe it. America had fallen in love with the charming man who had set the heartbeat of the nation to music.

The funeral was held at Fifth Avenue's Temple

Emanu-El in New York. Three thousand Gershwin admirers crowded the synagogue. Another thousand admirers—show business stars, musicians, policemen, waitresses, cabbies—stood in the gray drizzle outside.

Finally it was time to go to the cemetery, and the mourners started to file out. The organist began to play. Temple Emanu-El filled with the andante from Gershwin's own *Rhapsody in Blue*, and somehow the day seemed brighter. Even though George Gershwin was gone, his music was here to stay.

MORE ABOUT GEORGE GERSHWIN

1932   *Of Thee I Sing* was the first musical comedy ever to win the Pulitzer Prize.

1937   The David Bispham Silver Medal was awarded to *Porgy and Bess* as an outstanding achievement in the field of opera.

1973   The George Gershwin stamp was issued in commemoration of the 75th anniversary of Gershwin's birth. The 8-cent stamp was the first in the new American Arts Series and shows a profile of Gershwin with a scene from *Porgy and Bess* in the background.

1985   Congress passed a resolution that provided for a gold medal honoring George Gershwin to be presented to his sister, Frances Gershwin Godowsky, and for a similar medal in honor of Ira Gershwin to be presented to his widow, Leonore Gershwin. Duplicate bronze medals were offered for public sale.